Pieces of an Abstract Hart

Poetry and Exhales

Kate Hart Nardone

Pieces of an Abstract Hart (2nd Edition)
Copyright © 2023 Kate Hart Nardone

Cover Art: by Kate Hart Nardone and Beti Bup
Back Cover Art: by Kate Hart Nardone
Editing: by Charissa Ricketts
Inside Artwork: by Kate Hart Nardone
(Photographed doll sculpture created by Frederick H. Kramer)
Photography: by Kate Hart Nardone and Trinity Hope O'Brien
Modeling for illustrations: by Kate Hart Nardone, Trinity Hope O'Brien, and Kairi Mae Nardone

1st Edition published 2018 Red Dashboard LLC Publishing

All rights reserved. Blue Jade Press, LLC retains the right to reprint this book. Permission to reprint poems from this collection must be obtained by the author.

ISBN- 978-1-7374758-7-3

Published by:

Blue Jade Press, LLC

Blue Jade Press, LLC
Vineland, NJ 08360
www.bluejadepress.com

Forward

Written from ages 16-35, these are the exhales of the anger, hurt, grief, growth, strength, and redemption of my life. Though there are many negative emotions represented in the content of this book, I would like you, the reader, to understand that I am presenting moments of my past and heart with you. Only moments. Pieces. Broken or joyful, they were true of the time, and as humans, we have a right to those moments.

Several situations and individuals were the catalysts for the contents of this book. I am grateful for them all, positive and negative, for helping make me who I am today. I survived the things that I never thought I could. In fact, I came out stronger.

Most importantly, I want you to know that I owe all glory, honor, and praise to my Lord and Savior, Jesus Christ, for healing my devastated emotions, disappointments, and sorrows.

Whenever you feel unloved, unimportant, or insecure, remember to Whom you belong.
Ephesians 2:19-22 (MSG)

I pray that this collection is viewed as a testimonial of my true journey from darkness to light. May it bring you comfort. God makes all things new.

Blessed be the God and Father of our Lord Jesus Christ, the Father of mercies and God of all comfort, who comforts us in all our affliction, so that we may be able to comfort those who are in any affliction, with the comfort with which we ourselves are comforted by God.
2 Corinthians 1:3-4 (ESV)

I have included a Scripture reference with each poem (no matter the emotion) and the full Scriptures at the end of the book. May you see how God's Word has the final say in all circumstances. I praise Him for His wisdom and His corrections.

Blessings to you all.
In Him,
Kate

The following poems have been previously published:

"Primp Session" <u>Disorder - Volume 4 - mental illness and its affects (influence)</u>, TheWrite2Change Inc. - Red Dashboard LLC, 2018

"Monsters" <u>Moving Beyond Mars - Volume 1 - A Voice for Victims/Survivors of Abuse (domestic and sexual)</u>, Red Dashboard LLC, 2018

Dedication

I dedicate this book to my children. You have each brought light into what was once a very dark and lost life. You inspire me, heal me, and make every moment worth living.

Life can bring you down sometimes. People are going to break your heart and disappoint you. That is just part of life, and for that, I am sorry. If I could spare you every tear you may shed, I would.

It's okay to feel whatever you are feeling. You are not a robot. Be angry, be sad, be whatever, but do not stay there. Use these experiences as learning tools. Do not let them make you hard. Use them to grow!

Know who you are, and never forget it. You are strong, brave, worthy, unique, and cherished individuals who were created by God for such a time as this. You have purpose. You are gifts.

May you live a life of joy and wonder, and may you never allow the pain in your life to beat you. You are capable of anything! You are overcomers! You are warriors!

Matthew Devon,
Nothing is impossible for you. Nothing.

Christian,
You have always been enough. Always.

Trinity,
Never lose your fire. Never.

Kairi Mae,
Stay unapologetically you. Forever.

I am so proud of you. -Mom

Table of Contents:

Monsters	1
Labyrinth	3
Too Soon	5
Disposable	7
Unexpected	9
Splinter	10
Running Shoes	11
Friend?	12
High School Boyfriend	13
Liar	17
Forgettable	18
Little Girl	19
Hush	21
Female Judas	23
Opinion	24
Stench	25
Beneath Me	27
Illusion	28
Want You Here	29
Drown Me	30
Veil	33
Hereditary Sadness	35
Nothing	36
Mirror	38
Pity	40
Disorder	41
Done	42
Love	43
Run	44
Sleeping Pills	46
If You Really Knew Me	48
An Angel Among Us	51
Soul Sister	53
Letting You Go	54
Primp Session	55
Miscarriage	56
Games	57
Enough	58
Weeds	59
Move	61
Chance	63

Just Know	64
A Letter From Hope	65
Stella	67
Warriors	69
Goddaughter	70
Suitcase	71
Masterpiece	73
Glass	75
Grateful	76
Mother	78
Father	79
Gifts	80
Healing	81
This Heart of Mine	83
The Answer	85
Time	87
Scripture Guide	91

Monsters

Evil no longer hides itself
under bed frames or inside closets

It lurks behind smiles
kind gestures
familiar faces

It's an old man sitting on a porch
It's an un-raised feral child

It's in the atmosphere
thick, like smoke

It surrounds us
dines with us
walks by and says hello to us on the street

These are not campfire villains
These are the stories we wish we never had to tell

Our nightmares walk amongst us
making each day lived an act of bravery

Humans
the scariest monsters of all

God, help us

(Hebrews 13:6)

Labyrinth

Sometimes I find myself
in the midst of the action

Observing only
Listening
Watching

Soaking in the moments
Witnessing the reactions, replies, and emotions
that others put out into the atmosphere

Not judging or assuming
Just studying
Learning
Noticing that we all carry our weight unevenly
Handle our struggles uniquely

It's reality
Humanity

We decorate our souls
Close ourselves off
Regret vulnerability
Embrace who we are

We cause each other pain
We give each other strength
We build each other up with a single word
Or destroy each other the same way

Just rats in a maze
Laughing
Crying
Living
Dying
Trying to find the right path
Trapping ourselves
Making wrong turns

We search for love
We get let down

We get distracted
We stay still too long
We fear our own strength is not enough
to get us through
So, we follow others going the wrong way
to avoid being alone

We have different religions, beliefs, sexualities
Not any two people are exactly the same

We judge
We hate
We separate ourselves self-righteously
yet demand others respect us
for who and what we are

We fear, seek, curse, and deny God
all in one breath

We run from the light
avoiding the truth and exposure
of our dirty minds and hearts

Just walking contradictions
in a labyrinth of twists and turns
thinking we don't need a map

(Proverbs 3:5-6)

Too Soon

Missing you cuts deep
Messy
An undying agony
jagged and prompt to the inhales
of my every breath

Heaven deserves you more than I do
but I am bitter and jealous

Razor blade memories
Your funny faces
Our secret places

Tears fall like gasoline
burning my flesh as they fall
I'm walking a thin line
clumsy and shaken

I can't shake this…
The race of my broken heartbeat
The knot in my stomach
The feeling that I am trapped
in an unending nightmare

You walked into my life
as unexpectedly as you left
both changing everything

Everything

We were both reckless kids when we met
No ability to see
The future of our connection
The ebb and flow of our friendship

What did we know back then?
Black nails
Cigarette breath
Sandy feet
Salt-water hair

Neither of our lives
turned out the way we thought they would
But we were still us
still linked
still vital to each other

And one day you were just gone...

Without permission
Without asking those of us who love you
if we were ready to let you go

Knowing I'll see you again someday
when I say goodbye to this world
doesn't always bring comfort like it should

I miss you
and I'm impatient

(Psalm 34:18)

Disposable

Perfect stranger
Closest friend

I smell it on you…
the indiscretion
the hidden agenda

I remember your head tilt
the way you replied
with the tone of an infant

A clever disguise for sincerity
nasal and mocking
patronizing and gross

This is a sound I once trusted?
I found this endearing?
Was this once a love language between us?

Such deceiving sweetness
I'll never forget
and why would I want to?

It taught me much
your bag of tricks
the looseness of your lips

I replay your lies over and over in my mind
remembering how blind I was
and judge myself harshly
relentlessly

Cheeks flushed with anger
Chest sinking with embarrassment
Years have gone by
I still feel it every day

You were a coward
Not my friend

You used my brokenness
to gain something for yourself
and you did it with no conviction
showing me how disposable I really am

(Jeremiah 24:11)

Unexpected

It wasn't supposed to be you
Not you
Devastated and furious
How could you not know how important you were?

(Luke 12:6-7)

Splinter

You
A tiny shard
Instant relief upon your removal
Why didn't I dig you out a long time ago?

(Proverbs 14:6-7)

Running Shoes

The only person you fool is yourself
Spotlight shines brightly on selfish intentions

Little coward in running shoes

Their world turns without you
and has
and will

When you cross the finish line
the only trophy that awaits you
is the knowledge
that they made it without you
and were better for it

You were an incubator
Nothing more

(Psalm 127:3)

Friend?

A foggy haze named Sadness
invites itself in
takes the closest seat next to me
to have a chat

I can smell it
bitter and musty

It wraps its arms around me

The doctor says there is no medication
for this type of pain

No treatments
Not even a street drug

Regret is an eternal diagnosis

Sadness, my friend?

…I'll save a seat for you tomorrow

(Psalm 51:12)

High School Boyfriend

Temper-tantrum toddler
in a creatine-pumped man suit

Racist
Womanizer
Jock

"Can we be friends?" you ask
No, we can't.

Oh, you want reasons?!...

Let's start with the fact that
17 years is not long enough
to erase the destruction of my innocence
my self esteem
my identity

Or maybe it's the 10 years
of therapy I needed
to attempt to heal
from every disgusting thing
you ever did to me
Every disgusting word
you ever spoke to me

Perhaps it is because of your ability, in the past,
to convince me I was unworthy
Unworthy of kindness
Unworthy of acceptance
Unworthy of your faithfulness

Maybe it's because I can still remember
the feeling of your spit
running down my face
or the impact of your fists
Your constant threats
Your constant follow-through

Maybe it's my PTSD diagnosis
I can accredit to you

Maybe it's because I still cannot bend
the last three fingers on my left hand
I bet your Mustang still has my DNA
in the door seam

Maybe it's the broken blood vessels
in the center of my nose
that remind me of you already

See…
We don't need to be friends
I see you in the mirror everyday

But you don't understand why I can't look you in the eye when we
run into each other?
You think we had good times?

When?!
When you were constantly telling me
my friends were not good enough…
my style not preppy enough…
my opinion not relevant enough…
my personality not interesting enough…
That I simply wasn't enough?
That NO ONE would ever love or want me except you?

I was a child
and you taught me
that love was meant to be painful

Sociopath
Narcissist
Bully
You "Daddy-Issued" throw away

You showed me everyday
that I was worthless
And I believed you
and treated myself accordingly
for a very long time

The only memory I have that I relish
was the sight of you
punching yourself in the face repeatedly
when I told you we were OVER...
when I was old enough to no longer care
what you could or would do to me

The day I escaped

Thanks for that
Friend Request denied

(Psalm 34:22)

Liar

Did you ever feel guilty
Even once

Watching me hang on your every word
like it was the Gospel?

I slept soundly
I walked tall
I relaxed in my ability to be fearless of you

Ignorance is bliss

(Psalm 120:2)

Forgettable

A speed bump at most
No poem for you at all
Only a haiku

(James 4:6)

Little Girl

You bat your eyes
You, adult little girl…

Cry on demand
throw tantrums
act devastated by the aftermath
of the destruction that you created in the first place

Useless little thing

You juggled lives and hearts
letting all that is good and innocent
crash to the ground from your careless, clumsy hands

Exposed and pathetic

Game-playing
Adult little girl

(Proverbs 14:1)

Hush

Justifiable panic

Mankind is crafty with its hidden agenda
Its beautiful lies

You sold me a maggot-filled dream
dressed it up with fancy details
verbal, but empty

I soak it in
The poison
Your charm

I let it expand my hopes
until they become stale

Discomfort scratches at my door

I try to spit it out
the bitter taste of you
potent and nauseating
I need a distraction to cope

I create a visual in my mind's eye of what should be
Compare it to reality
Hate what I see

I act out secretly
but can't continue
because unlike you
my conscience convicts me

It's not so bad
It only burns a little
just at the back of the throat
Compared to the sting in my eyes
it's perfection

But you wouldn't understand that
You instead gravitate to mockery
Screw that

I'm just fine
…whatever that means

Departure is sometimes necessary,
but it's just as difficult as staying
Location change is irrelevant
if you pack the pain and take it with you

So, the thought occurs to me
Write this junk down
It doesn't matter if it makes sense or confuses
That isn't my concern

It's the noise in my head that needs to hush
My heart that needs to beat slower
and not get too excited
…just yet

(1 Peter 5:6-7)

Female Judas

I was never Christ
never pure and without sin
but I loved you
fully
unconditionally

You smiled and laughed with me
broke bread
drank wine
betrayed our bond for nothing
literally nothing

He was never worth 30 pieces of silver to begin with

Female Judas
opened legs
blind eyes
twisted heart

You invited the demons in
They can be your friends now

(Mark 11:25)

Opinion

Billions evolve over time
Experience, circumstance

And here I stand with this one view
unmovable
unshakable
and completely irrelevant

(Luke 12:7)

Stench

You have a stench…
Rancid
Vulgar
Lingering

Your soul is void

So well-rehearsed
you no longer need to review the script

You fool yourself
believing my silence is out of "fear of you"

Don't flatter yourself

Truth decides on its own
when it wants to present itself
So, I've released it to do so
My assistance isn't needed

"Truth"

Do you even understand that word?
Are you familiar with its meaning?

I imagine it's as foreign to you
as monogamy and decency

Do you not see the distance I create?
And then here you come
like a moth to the flame
only I'm the one that keeps being burned
because I'm holding
the only moral compass

I struggle
not to allow your dysfunctional weight
to collapse me
to the level of your pathetic character
that creeps lower than the cracks
of the filthy oil-stained pavement

You are where you belong…
in the arms of the blind
in the bed of the desperate

So, seek refuge and sympathy elsewhere
I'm all sold out here

(Jude 1:18-19)

Beneath Me

Predictable you
a bore
a yawn or two at the most

It's comical
magnificent
the clarity that time provides

I loved you?
The tiny, slimy creature that you are?

You're no more impressive
than the trash you pretend to be better than

We shared a cigarette once
You seemed ten feet tall
exhaling the smoke
and implanting yourself
into years of my wasted life

Screaming for your attention
like a neglected child
trying to save you…
rescue you from yourself
at the cost of everything
that was left of me

For what?
Turned tables
Slammed doors
Black eyes

I deserved it, I suppose…
to have my soul drained
my mind bruised
for loving something as beneath me as you

(1 Corinthians 5:11)

Illusion

There was a brief time
when breathing was calm
chest pains not as present
with each rise and fall

A time where everything made sense
but it was all an illusion

There is no such thing as safe
Life is a joke that mocks you until the end
watching you squirm in discomfort
and struggle to breathe through the pain

Moments of security always fleeting
searched for, but always lost
reminding you of how foolish
you really are
and have always been
for allowing yourself to believe
that you were ever worth the truth
worth the loyalty
worth anything at all

But, you're not

Deep down you've always known
Love is an illusion
and you're an ignorant fool

(Isaiah 41:10-13)

Want You Here

Distasteful jokes
Cigarette breaks
Angst with the world
Musical debates

I want to raise my voice
tell you you're wrong
that the voice in your head is a liar
hear new ideas you have for a song

I want to force feed you compliments
and listen to the sound of your breath
I want you to tell me
you'll hold on one more day
and not talk anymore about death

Speak to me
Cry, scream, say anything
Remind me that your soul is in pain
and I'll remind you of a God who loves you
when you feel broken, again and again

Tell me you love me one more time
and believe I love you too
Laugh — smile — crumble
Fall apart if you must…
I go through all these emotions too

Share with me your wildest dreams
and describe to me your fear
Nothing you tell me will scare me away
I just want you here

(John 11:25-26)

Drown Me

At night, I close my eyes to dream
then open them to join the light of a new day
The last and first of these moments
are always consumed with thoughts of you

They are both my joy and my fear

To possess the high regard
and genuine care of another soul
can be so uplifting
and so dreadfully terrifying
at the same time

If you never love me, I will lose nothing
If you never touch me, I will miss nothing

I am safer in my world of independence
where loneliness
is just a quick visiting enemy
that shows its ugly face briefly
but is easily chased off by distraction
of any and every kind

But love?
Love has a violent way
of wearing an attractive face
of digging through a ribcage
with no concern of the blood and guts
it eats through
to make its way into a heart
that fights vulnerability
like the plague it is

I look into your eyes
and drown there

My natural reaction is to run away
as though my life depended on it

But, when I linger there
beyond that horrifying
"Run for the hills" first second…
I can see myself in the reflection
and suddenly want to reside there
for the next 50 years or so

I guess joy and fear can co-exist
as a healthy balance

Maybe
I hope so
I could be completely wrong…
Probably

My point is…
I am choosing the possibility of happiness
even though I am petrified

So…look into my eyes
and drown me…

Please

(1 John 4:18)

Veil

What if just for one day
I tore off the veil
indulged myself in full honesty
and held nothing back?

What if people got to hear
the inner workings of my heart
exposing all the thoughts and desires
the lovely and hideous things
harbored deep inside?

Shall we dance, you and I?
Yes, you...
the one with no clue.
Would you be prepared
to soak in the truth?
Unfiltered?
It will fall like hail, I assume
cracking windshields of ignorance

Shall we sit, you and I?
Yes, you...
the one I secretly long for
Can you take a moment
and clear your mind?
Uninterrupted?
I'll expose myself raw
crumbling your walls of blindness

Shall we hash this out, you and I?
Yes, you...
the one who destroyed my soul
Would you be prepared
to shut your filthy mouth?
If not, I could sew it shut
and smile, watching it hurt you like hell
grateful to repay years of your violence

Shall we visit, you and I?
Yes, you...
the one I lost too soon

Could you fly down and wipe my tears?
Allow me to listen to your heartbeat, once more?
It would calm my spirit
refreshing my belief in God and man

What if for one day
people had to listen, had to see
unable to avoid the knowledge
of the admiration or distain?

Would lights turn on and redirect?
Or would all stay unchanged…
leaving me naked and vulnerable
veil at my feet
alone?

(Philippians 4:8)

Hereditary Sadness

Stare hard into the mirror...
the broken shards of glass

Who do you see?

Do not follow the footsteps
of his inner suffering

You have felt first-hand the agony it causes
You know the hopeless place it can lead

Your life is a gift, and wisdom would imply
that you walk a path less harmful

You can reflect his heart's goodness
remember his laughter and smile
but not repeat the wasted years...
not cause as many tears

The destructive pattern starts with solitude
Self-loathing
And you're walking full steam ahead into the darkness
purposefully hiding from the light

Please...stop

(Isaiah 40:31)

Nothing

There you go again
giving me the stare down

What can I do for you, Sir?
Is there something more that you need from me?

You've had my time
Wasted
You've had my patience
Worn
You've had my mouth
Tasted
You've had my heart
Torn

I can feel your eyes on me
Unnerving
I hear your thoughts loud and clear

What value does your life have without me?
Is that your question?
It's not for me to answer

See, I was all wrapped up in your promises
your dressed-up words
The heart is a fool like that
stays blind on purpose sometimes

But then I lost count
you know?
...of all the tears, I mean
And one day everything became so clear

Don't cry about me now
You never felt a thing
while I was drowning
just held me under further
smiling as I begged for a lifeline

Well, how about this?...
now I'll throw YOU a line...

But I'm not trying to save you, you see…
you've always been well-skilled
at pulling yourself under

I'll just wish you the best
but I recommend you keep your eyes to yourself
because when I look at you now
I see nothing that I want

"You are nothing."

…There's your line

(1 Timothy 5:24)

Mirror

The sting of all this loss
the choking grip of this solitude…
Will it dull?

It feels like fire
burning holes and eating away my insides
until all that remains of me
are ashes on the floor
that everyone steps over
and never thinks to clean up

I have no fight left
no longer even trying to be seen

Mirror, Mirror…
show me something other than me

Scars are souvenirs from places
I never wished to travel

The reflection comes back
and all I see is the outline of a ghost…
transparent and forgotten
mourning the loss of itself
its relevance
its existence

Mirror, Mirror…
I want to see someone complete

I hear the white noise voices
"You are so beautiful" they say
They say it and walk away
They say it but they don't stay

They never rip open the exterior
to look deeper inside
to see the maze of darkness
leads somewhere that light still remains

Mirror, Mirror…
show someone the inside of me

Let them observe the familiar and new
finding treasure in the decay and growth
relating to the chaos and the calm
enjoying the wild and refined
and feel comfort and excitement
in what they see

Mirror, Mirror…
show me someone next to me

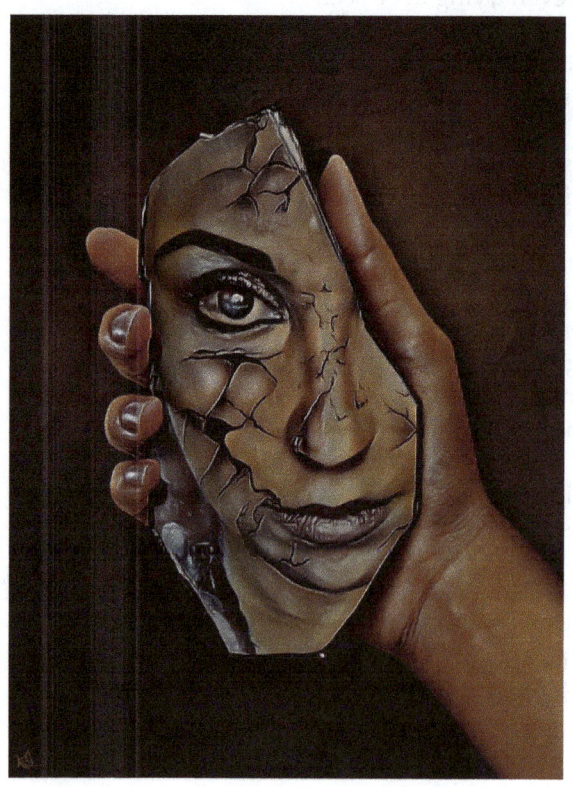

(Proverbs 31:25)

Pity

What's that like for you…
living life in reverse

Proving that everything you were
was as fake as I always knew it was?

You see life through a box
small enough only to view what you want
what you need

Purposefully avoiding the full picture
of everything and everyone that your selfishness hurts
while you are observed by tiny eyes with fragile hearts

Lust overpowers your love
Cruelty overpowers your kindness
Revenge overpowers your mercy
Desire overpowers your morality

Not one intention, plot, or game you play is overlooked
Where man cannot see your intention, God can
A reality, that in the end, you will not escape

And for that reason
my pain and brokenness for myself
is somehow joined with pity for you

(John 10:10)

Disorder

Where does my heart go when I suffer?

It forces itself from my stomach into my throat suffocating and nauseating me…

That's where it goes

(1 Corinthians 6:20)

Done

You always tried to make me question everything…
about myself — mostly
my tastes — my wants — my goals — my opinions

For a while…
I lost myself in your control and deception
too fearful of what might happen if I stood up
and finally walked away

So, I became a shell of myself
faking smiles
forcing laughter
holding back the gag reflex I felt
every time you touch me

I became void
Empty
Vacant
Numb

You tried to rob me of myself
and MYSELF was something I had forgotten I loved

Until that moment…
Why this moment, I'll never know…
but it started with a glance
This glance that was like so many before it
yet different somehow

That final glance in the mirror
Mascara running down with the waterfall of tears for the millionth time

I knew I was done

(James 4:7)

Love

I cannot matter to you
if you do not matter to you

It's over before it began

(1 John 4:8)

Run

Ingest it
your self-created poison
seasoned with your own manipulations
served scalding hot
from the hellfire that I'm sure holds your destiny

The words of your mouth burn like lava
melting peace and confidence

Are you relaxed with the notion
that your disguise is fooling everyone?
That it's made so well
others must pass by unaware
of the vulgarity and violence
that is woven into every fiber of your being?

But you are clumsy
Predictable
Soulless
Dirty

You can blame my departure all you want
but you were empty long before I found you
before I loved you
before I couldn't love you anymore

God knows I tried…
I tried to not stop loving you
but loving you was a prison
where I was stripped naked of my self-respect
my peace of mind

You pissed across the doorway of my freedom
marking your territory
like the dog you are

I felt it…
the cold
the panic

I trembled in terror of the lifelessness
of everything I was
and the hopelessness
of all I wanted to be

I became desperate for air

So, I breathed in
took a long deep breath

and ran with all my might

(Psalm 91)

Sleeping Pills

Give me something, please…

Something strong
Something quick

To quiet the noise
To slow the anxious heartbeats
To ease my swollen eyes

Let me lose myself for a while…
Drown out the question on repeat
"Why aren't I enough?"

Everyone wants something else
Someone else
Leaving me…
standing wide-eyed and open armed
holding my gifts of unconditional love
endless admiration
and laughter of joys yet to come
gift-wrapped in flesh
tied up tight with wishful thinking

I was beautiful once…
Less damaged
Now it's an unpredictable combo
of tough and crumbling

Which will I be today?

Distraction seeking me
Adventure seeking me
Peace seeking me…

To keep my thoughts at bay
Walking on ledges
Sinking under waves

It's all right, girl…

Someday it's gonna change

You'll lock eyes with a stranger
who will never want to look away
who will help you hold your balance
and pull you up for air

Your laughter will dance in their ears
Your smile will send aches into their bones
They will live, and love, and taste everything that is YOU
and they will know that they are home

Someday
One day

I need to sleep

(1 Peter 5:6-7)

If You Really Knew Me

You know nothing of me…
only what you believe to be true

You assume
but you don't see the daily mess
that swims around my head
Whispering
Screaming
Reminding me of the loneliness I feel
in a crowded room

You don't know about the moments
I question why I am even here
or why life just seems to happen to me
instead of me actually living it

Do not compliment or admire my strength
I'm just as weak as anyone else
Probably more

I get angry with God
I shatter things when I am alone
I scream into my pillow at night

My pain is real
It's raw
Cut open, time and time again
No time to heal
No mercy

I'm not "the cool chick"
Don't label me that way
I feel out of place everywhere I go
I'm uncomfortable in my own skin

Don't see my broken heart
as an opportunity to prey on me
to be your next conquest
I find more pain in realizing that…about you

I'm just a broken little girl
who wishes she could fly away
directly into the sun, if possible
evaporating the scars of this life

You call me beautiful
You have no idea how some days
the thought of making eye contact with any human
terrifies me to the core
Compliments won't change that

You call me a bitch
Well, on this we can agree
As loving and compassionate as I try to be
humans…especially fake "Christians"
disgust the hell out of me
with their lies and selfishness
their poor reflection of God's heart

Let my walls down, you say
For what?
So, you can explore and see what is left for you to take?
What do you want from me?
Confidence—Trust—Sex?
Something in common?

I'm sorry
That's asking too much right now
What you can have…
is the truth

(Psalm 37:8)

An Angel Among Us
(for Rory Wilson)

Bright Eyes
Soft Voice
Healing Hands
Contagious Smile
Beautiful Spirit

Pure, selfless, and positive
Leaving traces of light behind
every footstep taken in this life

An example to all
An Angel among us
whose flight back to the heavens
seems all too soon
to those who wish to have more moments
to hold you and thank you
to soak in your radiant energy

Knowing now, that although
you cannot walk beside me
you are watching over me
and the Light you spread in this world
continues to burn brightly
in the minds, souls, and spirits
of all who love you

Rest peacefully, my Rory
until we meet again
and we dance on the beaches of Heaven
wearing our wings together

(Matthew 5:4)

Soul Sister

Today I laughed
and cried
and felt you

I watched a black bird struggle to fly
and saw only myself, not you

I only picture you soaring

(2 Corinthians 12:9)

Letting You Go

Your spiteful actions
Hoping to press hard into bruises already made
but almost healed

Wanting the "almost" to turn things backward
and re-shatter my insides, the talented way you do

Wishing the damage to be irreparable this time
as if enough pain has not already been accomplished

You can throw your childish fits
You can pretend
I can't see right through the mask
you wear so clumsily for everyone else

I know everything you are
And more importantly…
I know everything you are not

I only wanted to help you
To encourage you
To save you
even after all the scars you gave me

But now I am letting you go

(2 Corinthians 6:14-18)

Primp Session

Good morning, mirror's reflection

Incidentally, I resent you
Your judgmental stare

The way you magnify and broadcast
my every flaw and insecurity so callously
like a spiteful ex-lover would

You look me in the eye
even less than strangers do

(Isaiah 43:25)

Miscarriage

Tiny fingers I wanted to touch
Tiny toes I wanted to count
Tiny laughs I wanted to hear
Tiny cheeks I wanted to kiss

Blood-stained disappointment
left my arms empty

You mattered

(Revelation 21:4)

Games

Skin grown over the mask worn so long
Was there a sting when it finally ripped off
revealing the real you?

Heartless
Desperate
Foolish

Juvenile justification
Grasping for straws
Voluntary stupidity

I might as well be the liar — right?
Since that fits perfectly into your agenda

Convinced you were always "the one"
Naïve

Wait for it…
One day the charade will drop

I warned you about his games
I leave you to your delusions

Enjoy

(Ephesians 4:26-27)

Enough

You are
You are
You are

No matter what you feel like…

You are

(Matthew 9:20-22)

Weeds

Masquerades
Chandeliers
Pretty things
Pearly smiles

An artful dance
masking tears
embellishing darkness
decorating gloom
playing pretend

Disguise it cleverly
this satisfaction
this "Plan B" life
that suits you so well

It's a skillful talent
thinking all is as it should be…
as it was always meant to be…
as you have been convinced it should be

Book smart, but in life so uneducated
So, the misfits creep in
and take what they need
leaving you clueless to the robbery
of your body
your mind
your soul

Sacrificing truth to believe
what is needed to justify what you have done
not to one, but to many

Living a guiltless life
You broke me into pieces
Destroyed secure places inside
and my trust in friends…humans…myself

But such a blessing it was…
unrevealed until the right time
when the sunlight of your absence came shining through

revealing all the goodness that can come
from removing the "weeds" of your life

I see clearly now
That was all you ever were
A weed

Previously attractive
I see now that you were just as dangerous
as the obvious poisons
that had been choking the life out of me for so long

So, along with the pain of your uprooting,
I have gained more room to grow

(Galatians 5:22-25)

Move

Reanimate
Swallow the failures and journey on

Limbo is not a place to reside
Time passes regardless
doesn't wait
is steady and faithful
to leave you where you stand
not able to care less if you join the movement or not

Your voice is stale
Eyes empty

I try to look behind to find you
I'm watching the image of who you were
get smaller and smaller

I have to keep going
I can't wait for you to live
and I won't watch you die

(Ephesians 6:10)

Chance

It exists

Heaviness lightens
Short breaths slow their haste
Troubled sleepers calm

Peace
Possibly
Maybe just a calm before the storm

The answer irrelevant
The truth revealed in time

Knowledge and ignorance
Walls and transparency
Work and rest
Doubt and faith

A collaboration of contradiction mixed
to create acceptance in a world so relentless

Creating one's own world
One decision at a time
One brick from the wall taken down at a time

Sunlight shining through
to places kept in darkness for so long

Hurt is always a risk in any openness
but so is bliss

Weigh the risks
It exists

(Isaiah 26:3)

Just Know

Always struggling to see the beauty you possess
that is so evident to the rest of the world

Never secure in the value and courage
you have welded into your very being

Fearful of inadequacy and failure
when in reality
you own every quality in you that the majorities lack

Integrity
Compassion
Generosity

Maybe you have been denied by others
these same qualities in return
and it has blinded you to the knowledge of your worthiness

Remember, know, and hold on to this truth I reinforce
every moment that I walk in this life
is a step I take stronger and taller because of you

No distance can change that reality
and no direction in life can defy it

Prayers — blessings — and joy
are wished for you always and in all things
For if you know anything at all
Know these words do not escape me in vain…

Know who you are
Never question it

Beautiful
Wonderful
You

(Proverbs 27:10)

A Letter from Hope

Mama,

I've thought about writing to you so many times. Choosing the right words to express my heart has been difficult. I was devastated to hear of the news about your health. The emotions that come from finding out that your mother is dying are hard to explain. I needed to reach out to you before the end.

I know it must be so odd to hear from me, being that we were never close (you basically forced my Father to take me). Living with Him has been wonderful, I can't deny that. He named me Hope. He smiles when He says my name. It makes me feel good. Loved. Although His love and acceptance has surrounded me unconditionally since the first moment He held me, I still feel wounded by your rejection. Because of this, I have asked Him a lot of questions, trying to understand why you and I couldn't have a relationship.

The hardest thing I ever asked Him was why you didn't want me. Even writing that sentence brings tears to my eyes. His eyes filled with tears too, as He explained that you were very young when you found out you were having me. That you had places you wanted to go and things you wanted to do, and that you felt like a baby was only going to rob you of those things. You were not willing to give them up for me. That was hard to hear. All I ever wanted was your love….

That is all any child wants.

You might not believe this, Mama, but…I remember things. I remember over-hearing you say you wanted to get rid of me. You called me a mistake. Yeah…I heard that. You made it sound like I wasn't even human. Like I was…nothing.

The last memory I have of being with you…we were resting comfortably together. I tried not to move too much, because I didn't want to wake you up. I heard someone tell you to relax, that it wasn't going to hurt at all. "It's just tissue," I recall their last words being. I couldn't figure out what it all meant…UNTIL suddenly…I started shaking around…and felt something grab me! I felt an agony I can't even fully describe…this sharp piercing pain. Giant metal rods tearing me apart piece by piece…I felt it ALL! Every cut. Every tear.

Every second of my panicked yet fading heartbeat. And THEN...I felt my spirit separate from yours. That was the worst pain of all.

...the next thing I knew, I was in my Father's arms. The God of all creation.

I'm not the only one, you know...there are others. Heaven is filled with us. Over the years, I have asked Him about their stories too. My two best friends here are Gracie and James. He said that Gracie was a result of rape. Had she lived...she would have been loved and raised by a woman that had tried her whole life to have her own baby...but couldn't. Her mother's painful situation could have been turned into a blessing for someone else. But...Gracie was never born.

James's mother found out that he was going to be born with a disability. She believed she was doing him a favor, not allowing him to live like that. He would have grown up to have been one of the most memorable world changing leaders in the history of our country. He would have sparked the flame that would have set the nation on fire for the Lord.
But...James was never born.

So many unwanted children, Mama...so many things that will never happen...because they were not there to do them. This realization frightened me...so I finally asked Him... "What about me, Father? What was I going to do if I had been born?" His answer? Mama, it's almost too painful to tell you. I was going to grow up to find the cure for the very disease that is stealing your last breaths right now. Me, Mama. When I found this out, I fell apart in my Father's arms. He cried with me and held me close. "So, I wasn't worthless, Papa?", I asked. "No, my beautiful Hope," He replied, "Remember...even My Jesus...the Savior of the WORLD...was an unexpected pregnancy too."

I want you to know, Mama...that I forgive you, even though it's hard...and my Father...He wants to forgive you too. He said that if you ask Him into your heart before you go, you'll come to Heaven, and He will give me back to you.

Praying I see you soon,

Your Hope

(Psalm 139:13-16)

Stella

My hero lives in a brown shuttered house
and smiles every time I arrive

She chases me with wooden spoons
Pretends she invented potato soup
Crushes on men with mustaches
Her candy dish is always full

She keeps my secrets
She worries
She forgives

She lets me be myself
Unapologetically be myself

She likes me

She gives me pennies for the wishing well
She sacrifices
She prays
She gives

She stands at the door of her brown shuttered house
to wave to me as I leave

Mother Theresa has nothing on my hero

(2 Timothy 1:5)

Warriors
(for Pastor Woodson D. Moore)

A leader of Warriors
You rise at dawn
Dress for battle

Helmet
Breastplate
Loin guards
Boots
Shield
Sword

You address your armies
Young and old
Equip them for the attacks that will surely come

The mission clear
The weapons of our warfare mighty

Salvation
Righteousness
Truth
Peace
Faith
God's Word

These materials make up the indestructible armor of strength
No enemy can overtake
No weapon can penetrate

Under your teachings we have gained
All we need to fight
All we need to overcome
All we need to win

An army of spiritual warriors blankets the earth
Because of your love

(Deuteronomy 31:6)

Goddaughter
(for Sierra Alexis)

I loved you before I even met you

When I held you the first time
I knew that there was a difference
between this love
and any other I had felt before.

An inspiring love

It was the first moment I truly realized
I wanted to be a mom someday

A jealous love
A fearful love
A protective love

You made my heart grow

(1 Timothy 4:12)

Suitcase

On a journey of sorts
Closed eyed
Listening
Hair pulled back tight
Pale skin
Hopeful

Caught up in a symphony
a tune that pulls like gravity
plants me down firmly
when I try to wander

An unavoidable painful pleasure
Shivers
Poison
Laughter
Despair

I didn't notice (as far as you could tell)
I didn't primp
only laughed at myself
amused by the secret
the pointlessness
tripping over the emotion

I'm running away
The grass is dying here
Throat dry
I've hit repeat too many times

Buy a ticket
Pack a suitcase
Search for something divine

Inhale new air
Feel the sun burn differently
Taste the salt of a new sea
and around the rim of a new glass

Bargain with strangers
Question everything

Decide what air
what sun
what salt
you can't live without
and draw a line

Rise each day
from the resting place you create
and live to free yourself

Show mercy to your failures
Renew hope for the dreams of your childhood
Allow shame to exit your soul

Let God flow out of your fingers
and light shine out of your eyes

Be strong
Be unrecognizable
Be transformed

Begin

(Matthew 5:16)

Masterpiece

Outside of myself at times
Reflections come back empty

I observe my surroundings
Tables
Chairs
Paint on the wall
Material nonsense

Is this all there is?
A daily dance of timecards
Polite gestures
Medicated emotions

Realizing the "fly on the wall" moments
are no different than the "wild child" ones
The feeling is always the same at the end of the day…

Alone

A guarded heart, still broken
Compliments and encouragement fall on deaf ears
Judgments and rejections shoot blankly
at a numb target

But when I pray…
God gives me a new outlook
viewing myself and others through a kaleidoscope
focusing on all the scattered pieces of
what and who we are
jumble and spin out of control

And I realize
that somewhere inside that insane mixed-up mess
there is such beauty

An abstract masterpiece
that doesn't need straight lines to define it
or soft brush strokes to be lovely

Because God takes both the beauty
and mess of our lives
and throws them randomly on a canvas
not to attract just anyone's eye
but to attract the right individual for us

So — I'll consider it a blessing
when I am passed over
because one day, the mess won't matter
and someone will find a treasure in me

God's masterpiece

(2 Corinthians 5:17)

Glass

Contradiction
Filtration
Distraction
Interruption

Accept or deny
the right to view oneself the way others do
Beauty to some is disappointment to self
Strength to some is brokenness to self

Half leveled glass
Empty with fear
Full of hope

Dance away the negative
Laugh away the rejection
Sing away the panic
Breathe away the past…
and if it shows up to torment the progress…
mute that noise, inhale, and move forward…not back

Seemingly impossible…
winning the argument I have with myself…
to prove that the violence — betrayal — abuse and tragedy
were character building blocks

But this glass
be it half empty or full…
is still mine
And I choose to add more hope
so, when challenges show themselves
I will keep it from spilling
with a steady hand
that has found its stability
in the circle of few who have stood by
with support and love

The few who have held me together
with prayers, and wet shoulders
The ones who have kept my glass from shattering

Isaiah 26:3)

Grateful

He struck my face with dirty fists
stained with selfishness and spite

She stabbed my back with a jagged blade
with a smile on her face

He screamed into my ear
shit-filled delusions of superiority
wreaking of greed and immaturity

I stumbled over my own bad judgment
shifted through the thick fog of disappointment

I abused my own temple
Cut deep into the pain
Purged to cope with the rejection
Closed my eyes and prayed for the end

I grew weary of this dark place
its monsters

The way they feed on naïve trust
wear well-crafted masks
prey on bleeding hearts

My impression of love...
always a motive
always a paralyzing word

Enjoyment on their faces
as they pull the strings
of us lowly puppets
twisting and knotting us up
until we are useless
hanging in limbo from our gullibility

You found me broken
clinging to the comfort of empty space

You cut me free
carefully untwisted the ropes and knives

lightly kissed the bruises of my mind
stared directly at the scars
and called me beautiful

You stationed yourself by my side
unmoving

You carry my baggage with grace

Your kindness drowns out
the voices in my head

Your gentleness heals my wounds

Your touch soothes me
where others have left me shaken

Your words comfort me
where others have left me terrified

You have the nerve to ask me
"Why do I love you like I do?"

I never even knew what real love felt like
until you found me

Everything I thought love was
you proved wrong

I am forever grateful

(1 Corinthians 13:4-8)

Mother

Life
Ups and downs
Rejoicing and sobbing

Your voice…a compass

Always pointing me up
Always pointing me home

(Proverbs 31:28-30)

Father

Not too girly
A God-created Tomboy

Bugs
Dirt
Reaching for tree limbs

Every daughter is a "Daddy's girl"
whether they want to be or not

So many feel transparent
because of absence or overlook

Not me

You allowed me to play like a boy
while reminding me how pretty I was

Those are the things that matter
Those are the things I'll remember

Your acceptance
Your praise
Your forgiveness
Your perfect reflection of God

Your love

(Proverbs 20:7)

Gifts

Energy
Creativity
Imagination

Carefully threaded together
these four small gifts
give purpose to my life

Fill voids and empty spaces
with joy and color

No more self-focus
Nothing else matters now
except the net of protection—I must weave
to keep their world secure

Realizing that I never knew myself
until the day they each made their way into my arms

Inspired to be more
To want more
To achieve more

Motivated to fight
Survive
To push hard toward a life
that would keep them safe

My sons
My daughters

My everything

(Psalm 127:3)

Healing

Like a cool breeze lightly touching the skin
I adjusted to the chill
the isolated hollow cage
I trapped myself into
expelling the frost from my breath into the air

Why was this so comfortable?

Escaping was as easy as turning a doorknob
and as difficult as swallowing razor blades
These bloody fists would not loosen their grip
on something so loved, yet so harmful
Logic lost every time, to a bleeding heart

Common sense makes a fool out of me
and laughs, and mocks and bullies
"Stupid girl! it says…
"You have loved so blindly
trusted so foolishly
ripped pieces of yourself off
and handed them over
to those who would never value the gift"

But change has come now
in an unforeseen moment
a split second of time
because I am ready and not forced
and that's how learning works

The cool air has become uncomfortable
the tight space now suffocating
razor blades palatable

The grip of my bruised ego
has finally let the pieces of my brokenness fall
leaving the decay of my love for you at my feet

I can feel warmth and sunlight finally painting my flesh
This must be what healing is

(Psalm 107:20)

This Heart of Mine

Pain

That's the reality of life sometimes
but it does not define

My heart—
My heart is something beautiful
something merciful

It's bloody

Dripping with compassion and empathy
for the souls that capture it
deservingly, undeservingly, and unaware

It rejoices when those held in it
smile with the slightest achievement
laugh with the simplest joys
or rise triumphantly
from the most painful circumstances

It aches when those it cherishes
suffer loss of love or life
struggle to recognize their value and worth
or latch onto something or someone harmful to them

My heart still beats
with rhythm and strength

And it WILL bleed with love and light
until it returns to the One who created it
just as He wanted it to be

(James 1:3-4)

The Answer

All the pieces of this broken heart
gathered one by one
by Holy nail-scarred hands
stained with the blood of mercy and redemption

Flesh torn
You hung
hammered by betrayal to a tree
that grew from the very ground you created

You traveled the earth
Wore the skin of a simple man

A walking vessel of Love
finding worth and purpose in the lowest of us

A slaughtered innocent
A willing sacrifice

Spit on and ridiculed
Mocked and humiliated

You took my pain
You took the pain of the entire human race

Of course, you understand my sorrow
Forgive me for forgetting

Jesus
Healer
Savior

From the ashes
I rise

No longer limping through life
crippled by the agony of the past

You made all things new
No longer incomplete or broken
viewing myself unworthy
You made me complete and whole
You were always the answer

(Colossians 1:13-14)

Time

I'm familiar with that pain
I've swallowed that pride

Felt the heat of unforeseen betrayal
flow through my veins

I've hated that which I once loved the most
Felt the rush of emotion so intensely
that my heartbeat could be heard
from miles away
Pounding and aching
Cracking and breaking

I've felt the terror of starting over
of venturing into the unknown future

It feels like failure
Plays head games of defeat
and intimidation

I've stood in judgment before many
Endured the whispered assumptions
The intrusive inquiries
The sincere and insincere
all feeling the same

And I've pretended to be fine

I've shaken my fists at the sky
Demanded explanations
A justifiable reason for this suffering
this excruciating confusion

I've cried and screamed face down
on the filthy ground

But time…it goes on, love
and your blood will flow evenly again

Hate will turn into acceptance

The heart learns to function
with the pieces that remain
It softens and opens again

The unknown journey leads to a better life
than the one you once mourned

The opinions of others fade into the background
mattering not at all

You will remember, after time
that God was there all along

You will recognize that the events of your past
although painful
have helped form you
into the person you were meant to be

You may not see or feel this now
Not yet
But in time
I promise
you will

(Deuteronomy 31:8)

God is greater than the highs and lows.

Scriptures

'Monsters'
Hebrews 13:6, ESV:

So, we can confidently say, "The Lord is my helper; I will not fear; what can man do to me?"

'Labyrinth'
Proverbs 3:5-6, ESV:

Trust in the LORD with all your heart, and do not lean on your own understanding. In all your ways acknowledge him, and he will make straight your paths.

'Too Soon'
Psalm 34:18, ESV:

The Lord is near to the brokenhearted and saves the crushed in spirit.

'Disposable'
Jeremiah 24:11, MSG:

For I know the plans I have for you," declares the Lord, "plans to prosper you and not to harm you, plans to give you hope and a future.

'Unexpected'
Luke 12:6, ESV:

Are not five sparrows sold for two pennies? And not one of them is forgotten before God.

'Splinter'
Proverbs 14:6-7, MSG:

Cynics look high and low for wisdom - and never find it; the open-minded find it right on their doorstep! Escape quickly from the company of fools; they're a waste of your time, a waste of your words.

'Running Shoes'
Psalm 127:3, ESV:

Behold, children are a heritage from the LORD, the fruit of the womb a reward.

'Friend?'
Psalm 51:12, ESV:

Restore to me the joy of your salvation and uphold me with a willing spirit.

'High School Boyfriend'
Psalms 34:22, MSG:

GOD pays for each slave's freedom; no one who runs to him loses out.

'Liar'
Psalms 120:2, MSG:

Deliver my soul, O Lord, from lying lips, [and] from a deceitful tongue.

'Forgettable'
James 4:6, ESV:

But he gives more grace. Therefore, it says, "God opposes the proud but gives grace to the humble."

'Little Girl'
Proverbs 14:1, ESV:

The wisest of women builds her house, but folly with her own hands tears it down.

'Hush'
1 Peter 5:6-7, ESV:

So be content with who you are, and don't put on airs. God's strong hand is on you; he'll promote you at the right time. Live carefree before God; he is most careful with you.

'Female Judas'
Mark 11:25, ESV:

And whenever you stand praying, forgive, if you have anything against anyone, so that your Father also who is in heaven may forgive you your trespasses."

'Opinion'
Luke 12:7, ESV:

Why, even the hairs of your head are all numbered. Fear not; you are of more value than many sparrows.

'Stench'
Jude 1:18-19, MSG:

In the last days there will be people who don't take these things seriously anymore. They'll treat them like a joke, and make a religion of their own whims and lusts."
These are the ones who split churches, thinking only of themselves. There's nothing to them, no sign of the Spirit!

'Beneath Me'
1 Corinthians 5:11, ESV:

But now I am writing to you not to associate with anyone who bears the name of brother if he is guilty of sexual immorality or greed, or is an idolater, reviler, drunkard, or swindler—not even to eat with such a one.

'Illusion'
Isaiah 41:10-13, ESV:

...fear not, for I am with you; be not dismayed, for I am your God; I will strengthen you, I will help you, I will uphold you with my righteous right hand. Behold, all who are incensed against you shall be put to shame and confounded;
those who strive against you shall be as nothing and shall perish. You shall seek those who contend with you, but you shall not find them; those who war against you shall be as nothing at all. For I, the LORD your God, hold your right hand; it is I who say to you, "Fear not, I am the one who helps you."

'Want You Here'
John 11:25–26, ESV:

Jesus said to her, "I am the resurrection and the life. Whoever believes in me, though he die, yet shall he live, and everyone who lives and believes in me shall never die.

'Drown Me'
1 John 4:18, ESV:

There is no fear in love, but perfect love casts out fear. For fear has to do with punishment, and whoever fears has not been perfected in love.

'Veil'
Philippians 4:8, ESV:

Finally, brothers, whatever is true, whatever is honorable, whatever is just, whatever is pure, whatever is lovely, whatever is commendable, if there is any excellence, if there is anything worthy of praise, think about these things.

'Hereditary Sadness'
Isaiah 40:31, ESV:

…but they who wait for the LORD shall renew their strength; they shall mount up with wings like eagles; they shall run and not be weary; they shall walk and not faint.

'Nothing'
1 Timothy 5:24, MSG:

The sins of some people are blatant and march them right into court. The sins of others don't show up until much later.

'Mirror'
Proverbs 31:25, ESV:

Strength and dignity are her clothing, and she laughs at the time to come.

'Pity'
John 10:10, ESV:

The thief comes only to steal and kill and destroy. I came that they may have life and have it abundantly.

'Disorder'
1 Corinthians 6:20, ESV:

...for you were bought with a price. So, glorify God in your body.

'Done'
James 4:7, ESV:

Submit yourselves therefore to God. Resist the devil, and he will flee from you.

'Love'
1 John 4:8, ESV:

Anyone who does not love does not know God, because God is love.

'Run'
Psalm 91, ESV:

He who dwells in the shelter of the Most High will abide in the shadow of the Almighty.

I will say to the LORD, "My refuge and my fortress, my God, in whom I trust."

For he will deliver you from the snare of the fowler and from the deadly pestilence.

He will cover you with his pinions, and under his wings you will find refuge; his faithfulness is a shield and buckler.

You will not fear the terror of the night, nor the arrow that flies by day, nor the pestilence that stalks in darkness, nor the destruction that wastes at noonday.

A thousand may fall at your side, ten thousand at your right hand, but it will not come near you.

You will only look with your eyes and see the recompense of the wicked.
Because you have made the LORD your dwelling place—the Most High, who is my refuge —no evil shall be allowed to befall you, no plague come near your tent.
For he will command his angels concerning you to guard you in all your ways.
On their hands they will bear you up, lest you strike your foot against a stone.
You will tread on the lion and the adder; the young lion and the serpent you will trample underfoot.

"Because he holds fast to me in love, I will deliver him; I will protect him, because he knows my name. When he calls to me, I will answer him; I will be with him in trouble; I will rescue him and honor him. With long life I will satisfy him and show him my salvation."

'Sleeping Pills'
1 Peter 5:6-7, ESV:

Humble yourselves, therefore, under the mighty hand of God so that at the proper time he may exalt you, casting all your anxieties on him, because he cares for you.

'If You Really Knew Me'
Psalm 37:8, ESV:

Refrain from anger, and forsake wrath! Fret not yourself; it tends only to evil.

'An Angel Among Us'
Matthew 5:4, ESV:

"Blessed are those who mourn, for they shall be comforted."

'Soul Sister'
2 Corinthians 12:9, ESV:

But he said to me, "My grace is sufficient for you, for my power is made perfect in weakness." Therefore, I will boast all the more gladly of my weaknesses, so that the power of Christ may rest upon me.

'Letting You Go'
2 Corinthians 6:14-18, MSG:

Don't become partners with those who reject God. How can you make a partnership out of right and wrong? That's not partnership; that's war. Is light best friends with dark? Does Christ go strolling with the Devil? Do trust and mistrust hold hands? Who would think of setting up pagan idols in God's holy Temple? But that is exactly what we are, each of us a temple in whom God lives. God himself put it this way:
"I'll live in them, move into them;
   I'll be their God and they'll be my people.
So leave the corruption and compromise;
   leave it for good," says God.
"Don't link up with those who will pollute you.
   I want you all for myself.
I'll be a Father to you;
   you'll be sons and daughters to me."
The Word of the Master, God.

'Primp Session'
Isaiah 43:25, ESV:

"I, I am he who blots out your transgressions for my own sake, and I will not remember your sins."

'Miscarriage'
Revelation 21:4, ESV:

He will wipe away every tear from their eyes, and death shall be no more, neither shall there be mourning, nor crying, nor pain anymore, for the former things have passed away.

'Games'
Ephesians 4:26-27, ESV:

Be angry and do not sin; do not let the sun go down on your anger, and give no opportunity to the devil.

'Enough'
Matthew 9:20-22, ESV:

And behold, a woman who had suffered from a discharge of blood for twelve years came up behind him and touched the fringe of his garment, for she said to herself, "If I only touch his garment, I will be made well." Jesus turned, and seeing her he said, "Take heart, daughter; your faith has made you well."

'Weeds'
Galatians 5:22-25, ASV:

But the fruit of the Spirit is love, joy, peace, longsuffering, kindness, goodness, faithfulness, meekness, self-control; against such there is no law. And they that are of Christ Jesus have crucified the flesh with the passions and the lusts thereof.

'Move'
Ephesians 6:10, ESV:

Finally, be strong in the Lord and in the strength of his might.

'Chance'
Isaiah 26:3, ESV:

You keep him in perfect peace whose mind is stayed on you, because he trusts in you. You keep him in perfect peace whose mind is stayed on you, because he trusts in you. Thou wilt keep him in perfect peace, whose mind is stayed on thee; because he trusteth in thee.

'Just Know'
Proverbs 27:10, NIV:

Do not forsake your friend or a friend of your family, and do not go to your relative's house when disaster strikes you-- better a neighbor nearby than a relative far away.

'A Letter From Hope'
Psalm 137:13-16, ESV:

For you formed my inward parts; you knitted me together in my mother's womb. I praise you, for I am fearfully and wonderfully made. Wonderful are your works; my soul knows it very well. My frame was not hidden from you, when I was being made in secret, intricately woven in the depths of the earth. Your eyes saw my unformed substance; in your book were written, every one of them, the days that were formed for me, when as yet there was none of them.

'Stella'
2 Timothy 1:5, MSG:

That precious memory triggers another: your honest faith - and what a rich faith it is, handed down from your grandmother Lois to your mother Eunice, and now to you!

'Warriors'
Deuteronomy 31:6, KJV:

Be strong and of a good courage, fear not, nor be afraid of them: for the LORD thy God, he it is that doth go with thee; he will not fail thee, nor forsake thee.

'Goddaughter'
1 Timothy 4:12, ESV:

Let no one despise you for your youth, but set the believers an example in speech, in conduct, in love, in faith, in purity.

'Suitcase'
Matthew 5:16, ESV:

In the same way, let your light shine before others, so that they may see your good works and give glory to your Father who is in heaven.

'Masterpiece'
2 Corinthians 5:178, ESV:

Therefore, if anyone is in Christ, he is a new creation. The old has passed away; behold, the new has come.

'Glass'
Isaiah 26:3, ESV:

You keep him in perfect peace whose mind is stayed on you, because he trusts in you.

'Grateful'
1 Corinthians 13:4-8, ESV:

Love is patient and kind; love does not envy or boast; it is not arrogant or rude. It does not insist on its own way; it is not irritable or resentful; it does not rejoice at wrongdoing but rejoices with the truth. Love bears all things, believes all things, hopes all things, endures all things. Love never ends. As for prophecies, they will pass away; as for tongues, they will cease; as for knowledge, it will pass away.

'Mother'
Proverbs 31:28-30, ESV:

Her children rise up and call her blessed; her husband also, and he praises her: "Many women have done excellently, but you surpass them all." Charm is deceitful, and beauty is vain, but a woman who fears the LORD is to be praised.

'Father'
Proverbs 20:7, ESV:

The righteous who walks in his integrity - blessed are his children after him!

'Gifts'
Psalm 127:3, ESV:

Behold, children are a heritage from the LORD, the fruit of the womb a reward.

'Healing'
Psalm 107:20, ESV:

He sent out his word and healed them, and delivered them from their destruction.

'This Heart of Mine'
James 1:3-4, ESV:

...for you know that the testing of your faith produces steadfastness. And let steadfastness have its full effect, that you may be perfect and complete, lacking in nothing.

'The Answer'
Colossians 1:3-4, ESV:

...for you know that the testing of your faith produces steadfastness. And let steadfastness have its full effect, that you may be perfect and complete, lacking in nothing.

'Time'
Deuteronomy 31:8, ESV:

It is the LORD who goes before you. He will be with you; he will not leave you or forsake you. Do not fear or be dismayed.

ABOUT THE AUTHOR

Kate is a 40-year-old wife and mother of four magical misfits.

Originally from Millville, N.J., Kate was raised by parents who loved God and each other, and who set a wonderful example of integrity and compassion to her and her sister Megan growing up.

Kate attended Fairton Christian Center Academy from K-12, where she entered and placed in several writing competitions. She then attended Cumberland County College where she met her mentor and now friend, Professor Kevin McGarvey, who helped Kate truly recognize the talent and the passion she had for poetry and writing. She later went on to receive her Certification in the Mastery of the Works of Walt Whitman from Harvard University in 2014.

An active member of the Glasstown Art District in Millville since 2012, Kate owned and operated her first art studio in 2013 at the Village on High, later relocating to The Riverfront Renaissance Center for the Arts, where she still operates today. She attributes her progress as an artist and writer to the unique community of creatives who have become her daily encouragers in all things that are dear to her heart.

Terrified of public speaking for years, Kate's first public poetry readings took place in 2012 at Bogart's Books and Café, a place adored by Kate and vital to her evolution as a poet. She thanks Rebecca Bonham and the members of Poetry on High for pushing her off the cliff of self-doubt and allowing her to free fall into self-acceptance and transparency. It gave her freedom.

Kate is a four-time published author with several new projects in the works.

This book is the second edition of Kate's first publication from 2018.

www.ingramcontent.com/pod-product-compliance
Lightning Source LLC
Chambersburg PA
CBHW071008160426
43193CB00012B/1968